PILLAR BASICS: *Grow Your Faith*
Establishing the Rhythms of a Growing Christian

TABLE OF CONTENTS

PILLAR BASICS: *Grow Your Faith*
Establishing the Rhythms of a Growing Christian

Pillar Church exists to *Know Jesus and Make Him Known*. We desire for every person that uses this guide to increasingly 1.) deepen their love for Jesus and 2.) devote themselves to *helping others* experience Jesus.

In short we aim to help Every Christian Become a *Multiplier*.

In this guide, we want to help you establish rhythms in your life that will lead to a growing faith in Christ. The mindsets, practices, and disciplines that help us grow do not change based on where we are in our journey of faith. They deepen and grow *with us* as we change and encounter the challenges of life; they provide a helpful framework to return to when we feel stagnant or need renewal.

The *Grow Your Faith* discipleship guide is designed to be experienced with one or two other people in a peer-to-peer setting. It covers ten primary rhythms of a growing Christian that include important passages of scripture, key insights, and discussion questions. Like all of our PILLAR BASICS materials, **we aim to equip you for Spiritual growth in three distinct categories:**

1. *Biblical Principles* that will establish an underlying theology of each rhythm that is covered.
2. *Basic Practices* that can help you envision ways to practically integrate the rhythms into your daily life.
3. *Being Purposeful* to maximize your specific experience in the life of your Church to help yourself and others to grow.

The best way to use the booklet is to see it as a *tool* to guide conversations about the topics in each session. After the introduction, the sessions cover **ten rhythms** or regular practices that help Christians experience and internalize the truths of the gospel. When you think about the rhythm of a song, it is the fundamental structure that repeats itself and brings together all the elements of the song. Similarly, these rhythms are the repeated ways we bring our heart and life to God and allow Him to deeply form us in Christ.

Throughout the study there are passages, paragraphs of explanation, and questions. The tool works best when you take turns reading the different sections, reflect on how the ideas are found in the passage, and answer questions transparently and substantively. To enhance the conversations, it can help to go over the session individually first before working through it together. This allows you to reflect on the questions and prepare you to process the content together.

Summary: When we become a Christian we walk through a door to faith in Christ. Our faith in Christ puts us in a new relationship with God that only grows as we experience increased faith in Him. What does that look like? Faith can look like trust, submission to His authority, patience as we wait for promises, devotion to the mission, and obedience to His instruction. One portion of Scripture makes it clear that *without faith* it is impossible to please God (Hebrews 11:6).

So how does our faith grow? In this session we will discover that *our faith is supplemented by a variety of different experiences and activities.*

> **2 Peter 1:3-9.** [3] His divine power has granted to us all things that pertain to life and godliness, through the knowledge of him who called us to his own glory and excellence, [4] by which he has granted to us his precious and very great promises, so that through them you may become partakers of the divine nature, having escaped from the corruption that is in the world because of sinful desire. [5] For this very reason, make every effort to supplement your faith with virtue, and virtue with knowledge, [6] and knowledge with self-control, and self-control with steadfastness, and steadfastness with godliness, [7] and godliness with brotherly affection, and brotherly affection with love. [8] For if these qualities are yours and are increasing, they keep you from being ineffective or unfruitful in the knowledge of our Lord Jesus Christ. [9] For whoever lacks these qualities is so nearsighted that he is blind, having forgotten that he was cleansed from his former sins. (ESV)

In order to understand the text, we will focus on the argument made in verse 5. The Apostle Peter gives instructions about: 1. what to do to grow your faith, 2. how to grow your faith, and 3. why to grow your faith.

1. What should we do to grow our faith? *Supplement your faith with nutrients.*

Here we discover that our faith grows indirectly as we supply it with the necessary experiences and commitments. These things will allow our faith to be nourished and grow. The overall focus here is on growing our faith, not on the supplements themselves. We don't focus on virtue, knowledge, or brotherly affection as the goal *in and of themselves.* They become building blocks through which our faith gains a firmer foundation and grows.

Q. What are some of the supplements that grow our faith that are listed in verses 5-7? Identify them. Write a sentence or discuss how they might lead to increased faith or trust in Christ.

2. How should we go about growing our faith? *We make it the top priority of our lives.* In the words of verse 5, Peter instructs us to *make every effort* to see our faith grow by making sure to supplement it with the qualities that we have just identified. It's interesting here because *effort is not seen as opposed to faith* **when it is fueled by gospel truths.**

We are saved by faith, we grow through increased faith, and we experience increased faith as we put effort into seeing these qualities produced in our lives. Notice that Peter thinks we will experience *resistance* in supplementing our faith. We won't be motivated to supplement our faith. So he gives us an illustration of what kind of life we will live if our faith is not increasing. We will live a near-sighted life (see verse 9).

Q. What does Peter mean by a "near-sighted" life? Why would it be a problem?

Q. How can you see evidence of "near-sightedness" in your past decisions?

3. Why should we make every effort to grow our faith? *Faith is how we experience the promises of the gospel personally and participate in a life with God.*

According to the passage, through Christ we have *already* been "granted" very great and precious promises. They have been granted so that we would become "partakers" in the divine nature. In short, **the promises are ours** and invite us into experiencing life like God's life. The divine nature is a nature of joy, love, purity, and community, which we were created by God to know and experience. We forfeited it through sin, but Jesus died for us to bring us back into this relationship with God. Why? So we could know and enjoy this nature again.

In short, we do not *"make every effort" to grow our faith* in hopes to **gain** the promises *but because we already have them.* Faith is how we take hold of the reality of God's life for us.

Think of it like this: When one of my daughters was young I bought her a Danish for the first time. With much excitement and anticipation, I paid for it and set it in front of her. But no matter how much I tried to convince her, she wouldn't touch it. The danish belonged to her *in reality*; it was hers! But it did not belong to her ***in experience*** *until she took the first bite (and never turned back).*

God has invited us to participate in life with Him; it belongs to us through our faith in Christ. **But only as our faith increases and we take up the promises *in reality* will it belong to us *in experience*.**

Q. Can you think of some promises of God that belong to you in reality but not in experience?

Rhythm 1: BELIEVING

Summary: The Christian life *begins* by faith in Christ and it *continues on to maturity* by faith. Much of the power of temptation comes from **not believing** what the gospel promises is true about us. So, one important rhythm of a growing Christian is actively believing the gospel in the everyday moments of life.

Galatians 3:10-14. [10] For all who rely on works of the law are under a curse; for it is written, "Cursed be everyone who does not abide by all things written in the Book of the Law, and do them." [11] Now it is evident that no one is justified before God by the law, for "The righteous shall live by faith." [12] But the law is not of faith, rather "The one who does them shall live by them." [13] Christ redeemed us from the curse of the law by becoming a curse for us—for it is written, "Cursed is everyone who is hanged on a tree"—[14] so that in Christ Jesus the blessing of Abraham might come to the Gentiles, so that we might receive the promised Spirit through faith. (ESV)

BIBLICAL PRINCIPLES

1. The *Curse of the Law* is a performance-based relationship to God. Jesus solves the whole problem of our situation described in the Old Testament. The Law of God contained blessings and cursing based on obedience or disobedience. To count on the Law (then) or our own works (now) means receiving treatment from God based on what our performance deserves. The result is that, despite some good moments or choices in life, we deserve to be on the wrong side of God's justice for the many times we have sinned and fallen short.

2. The *Blessing of the Gospel* is a grace-based relationship with God through Faith in Christ. Here faith or believing is equivalent to what we are "relying" on for our standing with God. Becoming a Christian means we no longer rely on our works as the basis for being blessed by God with forgiveness and eternal life. We rely on Jesus taking the curse we deserve away from us by His death and earning the blessing we need by His obedience. We receive the performance of Jesus as a *gift*. God relates to us based on the record of Jesus' perfect obedience both now and forever.

3. The *Righteous Shall Live by Faith* means that our relationship with God continues on the basis of faith. The Galatian church being written to here was tempted to view their ongoing relationship with God through the lens of the "works of the law" (see verse Galatians 3:1 and following). But through the lens of the gospel we see that God is working by His Holy Spirit to bring us into the blessing of Christ-like maturity on the way to Eternal Life...despite our failures *or successes*!

BASIC PRACTICES

1. Honestly examine the basis of your relationship with God. Many people have mistaken their religious practices for genuine faith. They feel that if they have been going to church or helping others or are generally positive about Jesus then they must be a Christian. But here we see that faith in Christ is a matter of what we are relying on for our acceptance before God.

Q. If you were to stand before God and He asked you, "Why should I give you eternal life?" How would you respond?

2. Rehearse the gospel in your circumstances. The best way to build a life rooted in gospel faith is to regularly stop in the middle of your circumstances and ask this one question: **"What is true about this situation because the gospel is true?"** I'll give you two examples:

"I feel like a difficult relationship can never change." Because the gospel is true, you can believe that God is growing you in the relationship and can help you learn to respond in grace. Because the gospel is true, you can demonstrate love toward the other person from now until eternity *whether they seem to deserve it or not*. Because the gospel is true, God has loved you when *you* have been even more difficult than that person feels to you right now.

"I'm experiencing career and financial success." Because the gospel is true, God loves you the same right now as he did when you came to Christ. Because the gospel is true, your position of influence is not for your glory but for the glory of God. Because the gospel is true, the blessing of this moment is an undeserved gift.

Q. What are some circumstances in your life that you need help seeing in light of the gospel?

BEING PURPOSEFUL

1. Meet with a mature Christian and ask them to help you examine your grasp on the gospel. Explain the main points of the gospel message. Show passages from Scripture that teach the truths of the gospel. Give a basic definition of the terms *faith* and *grace* as they relate to the gospel message.

2. Read a helpful book that explains the message of the gospel. A few examples to consider would be:

What is the gospel? by Greg Gilbert
What is the gospel? by Bryan Chappel
Gospel by J.D. Greear
Note to Self by Joe Thorn

Rhythm 2: REPENTING

Summary: The Christian life is a continual experience of repentance. As we mature, we become more honest about the depth of our sinfulness. As we experience life, God brings heart issues to the surface where we can *see them* and *turn from them*. We repent of sin as we begin our walk with Christ and maintain a posture of repentance as we grow.

Matthew 21:28-32. [28] "What do you think? A man had two sons. And he went to the first and said, 'Son, go and work in the vineyard today.' [29] And he answered, 'I will not,' but afterward he changed his mind and went. [30] And he went to the other son and said the same. And he answered, 'I go, sir,' but did not go. [31] Which of the two did the will of his father?" They said, "The first." Jesus said to them, "Truly, I say to you, the tax collectors and the prostitutes go into the kingdom of God before you. [32] For John came to you in the way of righteousness, and you did not believe him, but the tax collectors and the prostitutes believed him. And even when you saw it, you did not afterward change your minds and believe him. (ESV)

2 Corinthians 7:9-10. [9] As it is, I rejoice, not because you were grieved, but because you were grieved into repenting. For you felt a godly grief, so that you suffered no loss through us. [10] For godly grief produces a repentance that leads to salvation without regret, whereas worldly grief produces death. (ESV)

Psalm 139:23-24. [23] Search me, O God, and know my heart! Try me and know my thoughts! [24] And see if there be any grievous way in me, and lead me in the way everlasting! (ESV)

BIBLICAL PRINCIPLES

1. Repentance means "changing our mind" when our sin is identified or revealed. In the first passage above Jesus celebrates the "tax collectors" and "prostitutes" who have repented of their sin. He also complains about the Pharisees who have not "changed their minds" about the preaching of John the Baptist.

2. Repentance includes a growing sorrow for sin. In the second passage, repentance is seen not just as an intellectual exercise but the result of a godly examination of our decisions. The people in Corinth had wrongfully rejected Paul during one of his visits, but later came to see what a mistake they had made and were sorrowful. When we are genuinely repentant we experience some manner of sorrow for our participation in sin.

3. Repentance is to be sought with God's help. In the Psalm above, King David assumes there are areas of sin in his life that he is still blind to. He asks God to examine his heart and bring before him areas where he needs to change. He wants God to lead him out of ways that grieve God to His everlasting ways.

BASIC PRACTICES

1. Identify areas of your life where you need to change. Repentance begins with honesty. Sometimes we have areas where God is obviously calling us to make changes and we have refused to do so.

Q. What is an area of your life where you are not walking in repentance (you know something is wrong but have made little or no effort to change)?

2. Ask God to reveal areas of sin in your life where repentance is needed. We should automatically assume we are blind to certain areas of unfaithfulness to God. Regularly ask God to search your heart and reveal these areas.

Q. Has there ever been a time where you became aware of something you had been doing that dishonored God?

BEING PURPOSEFUL

1. Use the time during the Lord's Supper each week to examine ways that God is calling you to repent of sin in your life. The Lord's Supper is intended to be a time of reflection where we can acknowledge our sin honestly before God and do so with the remembrance of His pardon and forgiveness before our eyes and on our lips.

2. Do a word study in the book of Proverbs about the importance of receiving reproof, correction, and rebuke. Fill your mind and heart with the wisdom of God's word about being quick to receive correction from God and others.

3. Ask another Christian in your small group to help you make a plan for change in an area that you know you are being unfaithful. We often wait to address sin in our life until it becomes acutely destructive, but as God brings areas of your life to the surface it is important to act early and *get support*.

Rhythm 3: STUDYING

Summary: The Scriptures remind us that we are *required* to study God's word and *rewarded* when we do so with sincere hearts. Part of growing as a Christian entails growing intellectually in our understanding of the Bible. Without this sort of study we will lack clarity about how God's truth shapes the rest of our lives. But we do not want to just study the Bible as an intellectual exercise. We want the truths to change our hearts continually as we return time and time again to passages we thought we had fully grasped, only to discover there are new treasures we had missed.

Mark 12:29-30. [29] Jesus answered, "The most important is, 'Hear, O Israel: The Lord our God, the Lord is one. [30] And you shall love the Lord your God with all your heart and with all your soul and *with all your mind* and with all your strength.' (ESV)

2 Timothy 3:14-17. [14] But as for you, continue in what you have learned and have firmly believed, knowing from whom you learned it [15] and how from childhood you have been acquainted with the sacred writings, which are able to make you wise for salvation through faith in Christ Jesus. [16] All Scripture is breathed out by God and *profitable for teaching, for reproof, for correction, and for training in righteousness*, [17] that the man of God may be complete, equipped for every good work. (ESV)

Acts 2:42. [42] And they *devoted themselves to the apostles' teaching* and the fellowship, to the breaking of bread and the prayers. (ESV)

Psalm 119:9-16. [9] How can a young man keep his way pure? By guarding it according to your word. [10] With my whole heart I seek you; let me not wander from your commandments! [11] I have stored up your word in my heart, that I might not sin against you. [12] Blessed are you, O LORD; teach me your statutes! [13] With my lips I declare all the rules of your mouth. [14] In the way of your testimonies I delight as much as in all riches. [15] I will meditate on your precepts and fix my eyes on your ways. [16] I will delight in your statutes; I will not forget your word. (ESV)

BIBLICAL PRINCIPLES

1. Intellectual growth is necessary for us to love God fully. In the first passage above, Jesus includes the idea that we are to love God with our minds. The mind is where we think about ideas and discover new concepts. Study is required for us to wrestle with our understanding of Scripture and integrate the truth we discover into our daily lives.

2. Christians devote themselves to studying Scripture to become thoroughly equipped. The early church immediately committed themselves to learning from the teaching of the Apostles. What was the "apostles' teaching"? It was two things: 1. the explanation of how Jesus had fulfilled the patterns and promises of the Old Testament and 2. how we should now live in light of what He's accomplished. The New Testament preserves the record of the "apostles' teaching" for us to study ourselves. The result is that we can read the Old Testament with the explanation of the New Testament and be thoroughly equipped to live godly lives as we study and apply it.

3. Studying Scripture leads us beyond just thinking about God to knowing His ways experientially. The point is not to pass a written exam about the Bible, but to have our lives purified. The Psalmist speaks with language of experience that is built on a deep knowledge of God's word. Knowing God's ways, remembering His word, and being taught His statutes lead to a pure heart, a delight in God, and new vision for life.

Q. What are three ways you can observe the importance of diligent study emphasized in the passages above? *Write a sentence about each one below.*

BASIC PRACTICES

1. Read the Bible like a book. That may sound strange, but many people read the Bible like taking a dose of vitamins. We are tempted to look for a few verses that may be inspiring or challenging, but never read it for what it is: a library of writings. Make it a regular habit to read large sections in one sitting. Many of the New Testament letters are intended to be read as a whole and it will help you grasp the larger themes if you do not get lost in the trees.

Q. What parts of the Bible do you feel like you understand the best?

Q. What do you find most difficult about studying the Bible?

2. Read the Bible with a notebook. When you read the Bible it can be helpful to write down questions that come up as you read. After you're done, return and try to come up with a reasonable answer to the questions. Then move to using study tools that can help shed light on your questions.

Q. What are some times during the day that you could repurpose/redeem for the sake of studying Scripture?

3. Take advantage of technology to listen to Expositional Teaching and Preaching. There is an abundance of solid resources that will allow you to benefit from the study of others and gain a solid grasp on the Bible for yourself.

BEING PURPOSEFUL

1. Pay attention when God's word is being taught. Whether it is during worship on a Sunday morning or in another Bible Study setting, it's important to exercise mental discipline to get the most out of the time.

Q. What helps you pay attention when you're learning? *Write down two focus techniques for use when listening to preaching and teaching.*

2. Study the book that is being preached. Rather than just listening to the sermons on Sundays, read and study the book that is the focus of the current sermon series. Plan to read it several times during the course of the series and share the questions you have with those who are preparing to preach. You can also do the same with past sermon series by listening to sermons provided on your church website.

3. Ask a mature Christian what practices have helped them grow in understanding the Bible. Take some time to listen to how others have gained an ability to read and understand the Bible well. Make a plan to sit down with a couple of people that you respect and get ideas that can help you.

Summary: Jesus taught his disciples the importance of prayer and provided a model for praying that can help us develop a rich prayer life for ourselves. Many people get caught up in answering the theological questions about how prayer works *and neglect the practice of actually praying*. But Jesus teaches that **it's in the practice of prayer** that we learn and discover its value.

Luke 11:1-13. [1] Now Jesus was praying in a certain place, and when he finished, one of his disciples said to him, "Lord, teach us to pray, as John taught his disciples." [2] And he said to them, "When you pray, say:

"Father, hallowed be your name. Your kingdom come. [3] Give us each day our daily bread, [4] and forgive us our sins, for we ourselves forgive everyone who is indebted to us. And lead us not into temptation."

[5] And he said to them, "Which of you who has a friend will go to him at midnight and say to him, 'Friend, lend me three loaves, [6] for a friend of mine has arrived on a journey, and I have nothing to set before him'; [7] and he will answer from within, 'Do not bother me; the door is now shut, and my children are with me in bed. I cannot get up and give you anything'? [8] I tell you, though he will not get up and give him anything because he is his friend, yet because of his impudence he will rise and give him whatever he needs. [9] And I tell you, ask, and it will be given to you; seek, and you will find; knock, and it will be opened to you. [10] For everyone who asks receives, and the one who seeks finds, and to the one who knocks it will be opened. [11] What father among you, if his son asks for a fish, will instead of a fish give him a serpent; [12] or if he asks for an egg, will give him a scorpion? [13] If you then, who are evil, know how to give good gifts to your children, how much more will the heavenly Father give the Holy Spirit to those who ask him!" (ESV)

BIBLICAL PRINCIPLES

1. Prayer is based on a sincere invitation to communion with God. Jesus taught his disciples to address God as Father. By doing so, he reminds us about the nurturing heart of God that invites His children to spend time in communication with Him. The heart of prayer is found in opening our inner life in verbal expression to God. Through prayer we worship Him, process experiences and express our dependence on Him through requests. We do all of this from our position of children in His family through the gospel of Jesus.

Q. What are some of the categories we are instructed to consider as we pray? *List the categories found in verses 2-4 above.*

2. Prayer is learned through experience rather than intellectual study. The story in verses 5-10 may seem a little confusing at first. It essentially says the neighbor may not give you what you need because you are his friend, but will do so because of your willingness to ask with urgency and persistence. Should we conclude that God gives us the things that we beg for? That we can force His hand?

No, that's not the point. Jesus is illustrating how his disciples will learn to pray. They will learn to pray by *persistently pursuing God in prayer about the things that matter*. In doing so, they will see the connection between their prayers and God's provision and learn the Fatherly heart of God.

The one who doesn't ask **won't see** that they have received something from God.
The one who doesn't seek **won't have** the experience of finding God's answer.
But those who do ask and seek ***will experience the connection*** and discover the loving heart of the Father.

3. We should pray even if we don't understand how prayer works. Because prayer puts us in communication with God who is far wiser, more powerful, and of greater depth than we are, it can be difficult sometimes to understand the logistics of prayer. That's what we should expect! Think of it this way: most people don't understand how their cell phone can put them in instantaneous contact with people on the other side of the world, but they can still use it. We don't have to understand our phones to make good use of them, and we don't have to understand how prayer works to experience its power.

Q. What's your biggest question about prayer?

BASIC PRACTICES

1. Practice prayer as a discipline. If you find it difficult to make time to pray, don't accept a prayerless life. Like many other important experiences in life, we can simultaneously desire a rich prayer life and lack discipline in growing in it. It's important that we don't fall into the trap of hoping our desires will someday magically change and it will be effortless. Set aside time to devote to prayer until you grow to value it.

Q. What do you believe are your barriers to a prayerful life?

2. Participate in prayer with focus. There may be a number of times that you have opportunity to pray but instead you participate passively. Mealtime or even bedtime prayers don't have to be a ritual you perform just so you can move on to eating or sleeping. Times of prayer in a church service don't have to be polite bookends to our meetings where we feel obliged to acknowledge God. Engage times of prayer with a focused, sincere heart even if you aren't the person vocalizing the prayer.

3. Pray specifically enough to recognize when God has answered. Since prayer is an opportunity to learn God's fatherly heart for us, we should pray for specific things that we can write down and remember over time. Whether you write specific requests down in a journal or use a different method, learn to pray about things with enough clarity *that you can see the ways that God answers over time.*

Q. What are some specific things you want to pray for during this season of your life?

BEING PURPOSEFUL

1. Participate in corporate prayer times. Find out when your church gathers for corporate prayer and plan to participate regularly. Experiencing prayer together helps shape the ways that we pray individually. You will find yourself challenged by the sincerity and passion of others whose experience of prayer may be richer and more developed than your own.

Q. Who have you learned the most from in the area of prayer? What is it about their prayer life that has influenced you?

2. Consider taking responsibility for organizing prayer requests for your small group. Any small group would benefit from someone who advocates for prayer in their group. You can collect important prayer requests, remind the group during the week to pray, and celebrate the ways that God answers.

3. Read a helpful book that can give you ideas for keeping you prayer life fresh. Below are two books to consider reading on the subject of prayer.

Praying the Bible, Donald Whitney.
A Praying Life, Paul Miller

Rhythm 5: GATHERING

Summary: The Christian life is a community effort. Local churches are commissioned by God and exist to gather Christians together for mutual encouragement, protection, unity of mission, and edification. Gathering together regularly with other Christians in our local church is one of the ways that we are protected from Spiritual apathy and that we participate in the Spiritual unity that provides a powerful witness to the world.

Hebrews 10:19-25. [19] Therefore, brothers, since we have confidence to enter the holy places by the blood of Jesus, [20] by the new and living way that he opened for us through the curtain, that is, through his flesh, [21] and since we have a great priest over the house of God, [22] let us draw near with a true heart in full assurance of faith, with our hearts sprinkled clean from an evil conscience and our bodies washed with pure water. [23] Let us hold fast the confession of our hope without wavering, for he who promised is faithful. [24] And let us consider how to stir up one another to love and good works, [25] not neglecting to meet together, as is the habit of some, but encouraging one another, and all the more as you see the Day drawing near. (ESV)

1 Corinthians 12:12-20. [12] For just as the body is one and has many members, and all the members of the body, though many, are one body, so it is with Christ. [13] For in one Spirit we were all baptized into one body—Jews or Greeks, slaves or free—and all were made to drink of one Spirit.[14] For the body does not consist of one member but of many. [15] If the foot should say, "Because I am not a hand, I do not belong to the body," that would not make it any less a part of the body. [16] And if the ear should say, "Because I am not an eye, I do not belong to the body," that would not make it any less a part of the body. [17] If the whole body were an eye, where would be the sense of hearing? If the whole body were an ear, where would be the sense of smell? [18] But as it is, God arranged the members in the body, each one of them, as he chose. [19] If all were a single member, where would the body be? [20] As it is, there are many parts, yet one body. (ESV)

Revelation 1:10. [10] I was in the Spirit on the Lord's day, and I heard behind me a loud voice like a trumpet (ESV)

BIBLICAL PRINCIPLES

1. Sunday was dedicated to the Lord by the early church as a time for corporate worship and devotion. When the Apostle John is telling his story of how he had a special encounter with God while in exile on the island of Patmos, he tells us that it took place as he was in the Spirit *on the Lord's day*. The Lord's day was the first day of the week, the day Jesus rose from the dead. It quickly became the day that churches gathered for worship, studied the scriptures, connected with one another, and gave focused time in their life to the Lord. There may have been other things in life that had to take place, but worship had the priority.

Q. How do you think Christians today can demonstrate the same sense of priority for the Lord's day?

2. Gathering with the church is both a necessity and responsibility. It's common today to think of church as something we *might* engage in if we feel it benefits our perceived needs. But think for a second about the implications of Hebrews 10:25 above. We're *not to neglect gathering as a regular habit* for two reasons. First, without it we lack the encouragement needed to hold fast to our faith without wavering and stay devoted to love and good deeds. Second, without our engagement, others will be left without *our* encouragement for the same thing.

Q. How many plural pronouns can you find in the Hebrews ten passage? What do the pronouns tell you about the things Christians are to do together? *Write out each one.*

3. God has arranged you strategically to display the power of Christ in corporate unity. The arrangement of the church as a spiritual body with many parts is God's chosen design. It's *His* idea and you have a purposeful place in it that *leaves a void* when you are unengaged or participate poorly. The power of the gospel is on display every time we gather from all our different backgrounds and, as a unified whole, proclaim one hope together in the gospel of Jesus.

BASIC PRACTICES

1. Make participation in corporate worship the priority of every Lord's Day. In our cultural setting, Christians have such a long list of exceptions for being absent from corporate worship that it's hard to see whether corporate worship with the body of Christ has any importance at all. Consider your own practices and ask yourself what exceptions you have made and what they might communicate to other Christians in your own church. Being present is an act of worship in and of itself where we say to Christ and others that He has value that exceeds the other aspects of our lives.

Q. What specific exceptions have you made for missing corporate worship? *Examine each one to see whether you would repeat it in the future.*

2. Come to corporate worship planning to encourage others. As we focus on Christ, we are also called to tangibly *serve* and *encourage* the other people who make up His body. Our worship services contain people who may feel discouraged, are facing trials, have taken scary steps of faith, or are serving others sacrificially with little encouragement. Don't wait for *others* to care for the people around you. Come with a mindset of contribution and don't underestimate how even small gestures of service to others may meet a timely need.

3. Pray with expectation for God's gracious presence in the gathering. It's our desire that our gatherings be meaningful and that God would be honored with our time of worship as we sing, pray, and hear the Word. There are so many distractions that can happen corporately and individually that will keep us from experiencing genuine fellowship with God. Make it a point to regularly pray for the worship gathering and ask God to demonstrate His power and presence as we draw near to Him together.

BEING PURPOSEFUL

1. Ask another growing Christian to help you think of ways to make the most of corporate worship times. Listening to other people helps fill out our vision for engagement. We rarely have conversations that examine the thought patterns we have about important subjects.

Q. What is the difference between legalism and devotion to corporate worship?

2. Assess how your gifts, skills, and personality can contribute to the encouragement of others in corporate worship. *You have a lot more to contribute to the corporate life of the church than you think.* A great place to begin is to ask yourself these two questions: 1. How God has shaped me? 2. How could my gifts meet a need (corporately or individually in the lives of others you worship with)? Once you are done, pick two insights to act on.

3. Gather a group of people to pray for the worship service. Leading a group of people to gather before the service for prayer would have immeasurable impact on the life of the church. *Every church needs people who will **lead the way** and advocate with others in the area of prayer.* Pray for the worship team, those who will gather, for the preaching, for the Children's ministry, and for people to hear the gospel and respond in faith. It's simple and powerful.

Rhythm 6: CONFESSING

Summary: Sin has great power in secrecy. Many people work to overcome their struggles with sin by themselves mainly because they're too ashamed or embarrassed to speak to someone else about them. But *sin thrives in secrecy*. In the body of Christ we are encouraged to confess our sins to one another for prayer and support, knowing that ultimately Christ has removed the shame and guilt. Confession leads to freedom, support, and prayer that will assist anyone who engages in it.

1 John 1:5-2:2. [5] This is the message we have heard from him and proclaim to you, that God is light, and in him is no darkness at all. [6] If we say we have fellowship with him while we walk in darkness, we lie and do not practice the truth. [7] But if we walk in the light, as he is in the light, we have fellowship with one another, and the blood of Jesus his Son cleanses us from all sin. [8] If we say we have no sin, we deceive ourselves, and the truth is not in us. [9] If we confess our sins, he is faithful and just to forgive us our sins and to cleanse us from all unrighteousness. [10] If we say we have not sinned, we make him a liar, and his word is not in us. [2:1] My little children, I am writing these things to you so that you may not sin. But if anyone does sin, we have an advocate with the Father, Jesus Christ the righteous. [2] He is the propitiation for our sins, and not for ours only but also for the sins of the whole world. (ESV)

James 5:16. [16] Therefore, confess your sins to one another and pray for one another, that you may be healed. The prayer of a righteous person has great power as it is working. (ESV)

BIBLICAL PRINCIPLES

1. Confessing sin to one another removes the false impression that we are alone in our struggle with sin. When we look at the passages above, it's clear that sinful struggles are the reality of *every* Christian. Most of the time we're unaware of this truth because we're looking at one another's lives on the surface. In verse 7, confession is described as walking in the light. This leads to fellowship with one another where we realize we share a common experience in our struggle against sin.

Q. Are there areas of life where you are particularly struggling with sin? What would keep you from confessing them to someone?

2. Confessing sin to one another roots our identity in the gospel. We often want to present ourselves as *spiritually successful* rather than *saved sinners*. When we walk in the light together, it reminds us that our significance is not in our success spiritually but in Christ's cleansing mercy. We are objects of Christ's mercy and affection. He claims us as His own despite our failures. The true story is that our sin is great, but His grace is greater. He is most glorified in us when this is clear. Confession forces us to face our **false image** that we prefer to display and replace it with humility and compassion for others who struggle.

Q. What are some of the good motivations for confession that come from the passages above? *Reflect on them and write down three motivations for confessing sin to one another.*

3. Confessing sin to one another leads us to experience the cleansing power of the gospel. According to the above passage, confession is one of the ways our hearts are practically cleansed by the gospel's power. Confession helps us to apply the medicine, so to speak, to our real weaknesses and wounds of the soul. It leads to more specific prayers for victory and allows other godly people to pray for us fervently.

BASIC PRACTICES

1. Establish relationships with other Christians where confession can take place. Confessing sin to one another is best done in a relationship of mutual commitment to growth in Christ. We want to find people who trust in the gospel's power and learn to live honest lives together without hiding our sin. We don't need to broadcast our struggles to everyone, but we do have a responsibility to build a circle of people who know us and can challenge us.

Q. Who do you have in your life currently that fits the description above? Are they present in your life or easily kept at a distance?

2. Establish a pattern of transparency with other Christians. It's easy to fall into a pattern of fake relationships. Resist the temptation to put on an act around other Christians. It doesn't benefit anyone when we all pretend to be doing "just fine," *while secretly discouraged in battling temptation.* If we will just be transparent, others will eventually feel that freedom too. They will benefit from walking in the light in the body of Christ. The key is that we regularly pray for one another, guard one another, and keep our hearts free from self-righteousness by dwelling on the gospel for ourselves.

3. Tell your church leaders where you need specific grow. Church leaders are committed to helping people grow in areas of need. They are also best positioned to know the resources to help with specific problems.

1. Involve yourself in a small group or some other setting where you can establish relationships of trust. Staying on the fringe will *not* lead to real relationships. In most churches, there are multiple environments where you can find people to grow with where confession of sin is normal.

Q. Are you involved in any groups where transparent relationships can form?

2. Make confession a structured part of meeting with other Christians rather than an exception. For example, as you go through this study, make confession a regular part of your time together. Ask the hard questions. "Is there any sin in your life that needs confession? How can I pray for you and your temptations?" When we don't plan to make space for these conversations, it actually makes it more difficult to shift gears and bring it up.

Q. What are some questions you could ask one another regularly for a spiritual checkup?

Rhythm 7: FORGIVING

Summary: We have relationship with God because He has forgiven us. God is celebrated all throughout Scripture because of His willingness to forgive even the worst of sins. It's natural that, as we are called into His family by the gospel, He would instruct us to imitate His forgiveness with those who sin against us.

Matthew 18:21-35. [21] Then Peter came up and said to him, "Lord, how often will my brother sin against me, and I forgive him? As many as seven times?" [22] Jesus said to him, "I do not say to you seven times, but seventy-seven times. [23] "Therefore the kingdom of heaven may be compared to a king who wished to settle accounts with his servants. [24] When he began to settle, one was brought to him who owed him ten thousand talents. [25] And since he could not pay, his master ordered him to be sold, with his wife and children and all that he had, and payment to be made. [26] So the servant fell on his knees, imploring him, 'Have patience with me, and I will pay you everything.' [27] And out of pity for him, the master of that servant released him and forgave him the debt. [28] But when that same servant went out, he found one of his fellow servants who owed him a hundred denarii, and seizing him, he began to choke him, saying, 'Pay what you owe.' [29] So his fellow servant fell down and pleaded with him, 'Have patience with me, and I will pay you.' [30] He refused and went and put him in prison until he should pay the debt. [31] When his fellow servants saw what had taken place, they were greatly distressed, and they went and reported to their master all that had taken place. [32] Then his master summoned him and said to him, 'You wicked servant! I forgave you all that debt because you pleaded with me. [33] And should not you have had mercy on your fellow servant, as I had mercy on you?' [34] And in anger his master delivered him to the jailers, until he should pay all his debt. [35] So also my heavenly Father will do to every one of you, if you do not forgive your brother from your heart." (ESV)

BIBLICAL PRINCIPLES

1. Our willingness to forgive is a measurement of our understanding of the gospel.
Let's go right to the most difficult part of this passage. The best way to understand what Jesus is warning us about (the failure to be people who forgive) is to understand the underlying logic of the story. The person who has been offered such grace cannot logically do what the foolish servant did; they have not grasped the massive grace they have been given. Jesus uses the story to illustrate that *we have not wrestled with the reality of our sin deeply enough and turned to God for Salvation by grace if we refuse to forgive others.* Receiving the gospel *will lead* to ongoing change in our willingness to forgive others or we have missed the point entirely.

Q. What do you find most difficult about forgiveness? How does the passage above speak to that difficulty?

2. When seen properly, the call for us to forgive others is *small* in comparison to the forgiveness we have received from God. At the heart of this parable is a comparison.

God's forgiveness of us and the depth of our sin is compared with *our need to forgive others and the depth of their sin*. In the Parable, the debt forgiven by the King is astronomically large. It's an amount that no person could have paid in his or her lifetime. The amount the forgiven servant was owed is nothing in comparison to the debt he was now trying to collect.

Our lack of forgiveness toward others is seen in the same light. God has forgiven us of a more costly debt and paid it with the precious blood of His perfectly obedient son for our redemption. **Anything we face will fall short of that cost as we are called to forgive others.**

Q. What do you appreciate most about God's forgiveness? What's something in your life you're amazed God has forgiven?

3. Christians are to always prepare their hearts to forgive those who have sinned against them. This is exactly the point Jesus is making to Peter about forgiveness. There is never a time when a Christian should not be prepared to forgive someone who has wronged them. There's no number of offenses that can be reached at which point we are free from displaying mercy. When we are struggling to have a heart of forgiveness, it's time to go back to the cross and remember that costly sacrifice of Christ. We are to trust His reconciling power to enable genuine heartfelt forgiveness for the good of one another.

BASIC PRACTICES

1. Examine your life for unforgiveness. We have all experienced past hurts and offenses that we are tempted to ignore. We may not always be able to revisit the relationship with people in a way that restores it and allows it to experience the renewal of genuine love. But it's important that we take these situations and people before the cross of Jesus and examine the posture of our heart toward them.

If you can't rejoice when others rejoice, if you feel secret satisfaction when another person goes through difficulty, or if you can't imagine joyfully blessing their life in some manner, then it's important to search your heart with the gospel of Jesus. Jesus spoke peace into our life and invited us to be reconciled when we had abandoned Him. We must consider the ways that we can **imitate** His abundant grace and mercy.

Q. Can you think of people in your life you need to prepare to forgive? Are there past hurts that you've ignored rather than processed with the gospel? *Identify them and begin to communicate with Christ about the situation in prayer.*

2. Establish a pattern in your home and relationships of asking for and granting forgiveness. It is amazing how many people growing up never heard their family apologize and forgive offenses in the home. As Christians, this should never be true of us. Making forgiveness *explicit* helps everyone rejoice in the gospel rather than shroud it with confusion. Having conversations that address the ways we **sin against** and **forgive** one another help us to **confront our own self-righteousness, practice humility, and trust in Christ.**

Q. Are there situations in your life where you need to seek forgiveness from someone else? Have you ignored some relationship hindering offenses and just moved on? *Identify them and begin to communicate with Christ about the situation in prayer.*

BEING PURPOSEFUL

1. Encourage a forgiving spirit in the church. As a community of believers, we're prone to get offended by one another more often than we'd like to admit. When someone shares with you how another member or attender has hurt them, respond in ways that encourage forgiveness and considers that person in the best light. Then ask a simple question, "What do you need to do to be able to forgive them?"

2. Discuss any situations identified above with a mature Christian friend and make a plan for action. Without turning the situations in your life into gossip (maybe remove the names and consider how to communicate discreetly), talk through a plan to pursue the right course of action in light of what you learned in this session.

Q. What are some of the challenges involved in pursuing forgiveness in the relationships you identified?

3. Consider the topic further by listening to the sermon at the link listed below.
https://vimeo.com/228587105

Rhythm 8: EVANGELIZING

Summary: We cannot keep the gospel of Jesus to ourselves. No matter what challenges may exist in sharing it, the gospel is the power of God for our Salvation and the Salvation of others. Jesus has commissioned us to share it and without it people cannot call on the Lord for Salvation. We who have received this gift from God are now commissioned to carry it to others and called to go to great lengths to do so.

Matthew 28:18-20. [18] And Jesus came and said to them, "All authority in heaven and on earth has been given to me. [19] Go therefore and make disciples of all nations, baptizing them in the name of the Father and of the Son and of the Holy Spirit, [20] teaching them to observe all that I have commanded you. And behold, I am with you always, to the end of the age." (ESV)

Romans 10:10-17. [10] For with the heart one believes and is justified, and with the mouth one confesses and is saved. [11] For the Scripture says, "Everyone who believes in him will not be put to shame." [12] For there is no distinction between Jew and Greek; for the same Lord is Lord of all, bestowing his riches on all who call on him. [13] For "everyone who calls on the name of the Lord will be saved." [14] How then will they call on him in whom they have not believed? And how are they to believe in him of whom they have never heard? And how are they to hear without someone preaching? [15] And how are they to preach unless they are sent? As it is written, "How beautiful are the feet of those who preach the good news!" [16] But they have not all obeyed the gospel. For Isaiah says, "Lord, who has believed what he has heard from us?" [17] So faith comes from hearing, and hearing through the word of Christ. (ESV)

1 Corinthians 9:19-23. [19] For though I am free from all, I have made myself a servant to all, that I might win more of them. [20] To the Jews I became as a Jew, in order to win Jews. To those under the law I became as one under the law (though not being myself under the law) that I might win those under the law. [21] To those outside the law I became as one outside the law (not being outside the law of God but under the law of Christ) that I might win those outside the law. [22] To the weak I became weak, that I might win the weak. I have become all things to all people, that by all means I might save some. [23] I do it all for the sake of the gospel, that I may share with them in its blessings. (ESV)

BIBLICAL PRINCIPLES

1. We have been given the task to carry the gospel to those who have not yet believed. The first passage above is commonly known as the Great Commission. In it Jesus instructs His people to go and make disciples of those who have not yet heard and believed. It is a task that calls for *effort on our part* to join God in the mission. This mission is reconciling lost people to God by announcing the good news that Jesus has brought us peace with God. Evangelizing means "announcing this good news" and helping others know and follow Christ by faith.

Q. What do you find most difficult about sharing the gospel with people? Have you ever shared your faith with someone?

2. We must be active in sharing the gospel if people are going to hear it and be saved. In Romans 10:13 (above) we hear the good news that anyone who calls on the name of the Lord can be saved from their sin and brought into the riches of God's grace through faith in Jesus.

Next, the passage reminds us that to call on the Lord, one must hear and understand the good news of Jesus. In order for one to hear this good news, *we must preach it* (not just formally but in informal conversation). If we're going to preach it, we're going to have to go where they are. People hearing the gospel and calling on the name of the Lord will not happen by *accident* and we are the people assigned to actively pursue others with this message.

Q. Do you believe that many of the people in your community have a clear understanding of the gospel? What misconceptions do you think non-Christians have about Christianity?

3. We're instructed to adjust our lives to meet people where they're at in sharing the gospel. In case we've missed how important the task of evangelizing others is, the Apostle Paul describes his effort in 1 Corinthians 9. He tells us that he's made huge adjustments to his life to fit in many different settings to offer a meaningful witness to the work of Christ.

The heart of his instruction is summed up when he exclaims, "I have become all things to all people, that by all means I might save some." Paul strips himself of his own preferences and enters into the lives of others in meaningful ways for the advancement of the gospel. That is the example we are to follow!

Q. What would it look like for you to become "all things to all people"? What are some of the adjustments you would need to make to enter into more meaningful conversation with non-Christians?

BASIC PRACTICES

1. Pray specifically for God to use you in evangelism. We need to pray specifically for *opportunities to share the gospel* and for the *boldness* to step out and have the conversation. We also need to pray specifically for the people God has placed in our lives; they are the best starting point for evangelism. Don't forget that the power and authority of the message come from Christ. We're not alone in our efforts to share the gospel; we're accompanied by the power and work of the Holy Spirit.

Q: Have you ever prayed specifically, "God use me to bring (insert name) to you?"

2. Prepare yourself with gospel knowledge and conversation tactics. Many people have a weak grasp of the gospel. They can recognize it when someone else is explaining it, but they cannot explain it themselves. Others have a good grasp on the gospel, but are easily shut down in conversation from lack of confidence and experience in conversing with others about challenging topics. Learning to explain the gospel effectively is critical. Also, learning good conversation tactics will help you maneuver in conversations and put others at ease when you dialogue.

Q. What are common ways people shut down conversations about faith and make it difficult to share the gospel effectively?

3. Position yourself for gospel sharing by being involved in the lives of non-Christians. Over time, many Christians surround themselves more and more with other Christians. *Eventually they are not positioned to interact with people who don't know Christ* and so have very few opportunities to share their faith. If that is you, it will be important to think about how you can make adjustments to your life and reposition it for the sake of the gospel.

Q: What are the names of three people you interact with regularly that you can begin to pray for and share the gospel with?

BEING PURPOSEFUL

1. Participate in church outreach events and purposefully connect with non-Christians. Our churches do multiple outreach events throughout the year that serve the community in meaningful ways. For the events to be fruitful we need to go beyond having logistical volunteers. We need more people who will come to the events and *use the opportunity to* **connect** *with the people there and* **share the gospel.**

2. Make a strategy in your small group to reach out to people in the neighborhood where you meet. Sometimes the mission feels so large, we feel paralyzed. As a Life Group, it can be a community effort to learn how to meet people in the neighborhood and figure out how to share the gospel with them. Learn together and use regular time in your gatherings to strategize together.

3. Learn the names of as many of your neighbors as possible and begin to pray for their Salvation. Keep a journal or chart of your block and write names down. Commit to praying for them and building into their lives. Ask God regularly to open opportunities to share the gospel with them.

Q. What are the names of some of your neighbors?

4. Read *Tactics: A Game Plan for Discussing Your Christian Convictions* **by Greg Koukl.**

Rhythm 9: SENDING

Summary: The mission of the church is to continue to see the gospel spread and the church established among all nations as a witness to the gospel of Christ. The task of missions is too great for any one Christian to accomplish by himself. It requires working together with other Christians in a local church to send others to places beyond the reach of our daily lives. Simply put, we cannot obey the Great Commission individually without working together with the church corporately in sending and going.

Luke 24:45-49. [45] Then he opened their minds to understand the Scriptures, [46] and said to them, "Thus it is written, that the Christ should suffer and on the third day rise from the dead, [47] and that repentance for the forgiveness of sins should be proclaimed in his name to all nations, beginning from Jerusalem. [48] You are witnesses of these things. [49] And behold, I am sending the promise of my Father upon you. But stay in the city until you are clothed with power from on high." (ESV)

Philippians 4:10-18. [10] I rejoiced in the Lord greatly that now at length you have revived your concern for me. You were indeed concerned for me, but you had no opportunity. [11] Not that I am speaking of being in need, for I have learned in whatever situation I am to be content. [12] I know how to be brought low, and I know how to abound. In any and every circumstance, I have learned the secret of facing plenty and hunger, abundance and need. [13] I can do all things through him who strengthens me. [14] Yet it was kind of you to share my trouble. [15] And you Philippians yourselves know that in the beginning of the gospel, when I left Macedonia, no church entered into partnership with me in giving and receiving, except you only. [16] Even in Thessalonica you sent me help for my needs once and again. [17] Not that I seek the gift, but I seek the fruit that increases to your credit. [18] I have received full payment, and more. I am well supplied, having received from Epaphroditus the gifts you sent, a fragrant offering, a sacrifice acceptable and pleasing to God. (ESV)

Romans 10:14-15. [14] How then will they call on him in whom they have not believed? And how are they to believe in him of whom they have never heard? And how are they to hear without someone preaching? [15] And how are they to preach unless they are sent? As it is written, "How beautiful are the feet of those who preach the good news!" (ESV)

BIBLICAL PRINCIPLES

1. The specific task of the Great Commission is a thriving church among "all people groups". In Luke 24 we read another of the Great Commission passages where Jesus gives the church its assignment: to proclaim the message of repentance and forgiveness (through Christ's suffering on the cross on our behalf). It also says the message should be proclaimed to all nations. The term 'nations' may cause us to think in terms of geo-political countries but the underlying word has the meaning of every ethnicity or people group.

The gospel of Jesus is to be preached. As a result, a thriving witness is to be established within every group of people for whom there may be a significant barrier of language and culture. The commission of Jesus then is not just to reach *more people* but rather to bring Salvation to *every people*.

Q. How do language and culture pose significant barriers to the spread of the message of Jesus Christ? *Write down three possible ways these barriers would pose a problem.*

2. More gospel workers can go when there are more Christians ready to support them well. The Apostle Paul was helped in multiple ways by the Philippians church. Later in writing to the church in Rome he asks the question, "How are they to preach unless they are sent?" The question is practical and reminds us that the role of sending is as critical to the task as going.

3. Christians should work together through their local church to support and send Great Commission workers. The local church has both the privilege and responsibility of participating in the work Jesus left for them. In the second passage above, Paul is writing to the Christians that make up the church at Philippi and thanking them for the ways they have sent and partnered with him. He mentions that they have supplied Him with resources and sent Him short-term workers to support His current effort.

Here's the point: as Christians we can obey the Great Commission in one of two ways. We can *go* or we can *send*. Inactivity is not an option. The key insight in Philippians 4 is that many people have contributed and the gospel is spreading.

Q. What are some ways that individual Christians can become more personally involved in sending gospel workers? *List three ideas below.*

BASIC PRACTICES

1. Participate in a church that understands the Great Commission as a call to plant churches among every people group. If the explanation of the Great Commission above is true, then it does not make sense to be a part of a church that does not understand the mission that Jesus gave his people. You will be cut off from the sort of partnerships where real sending is happening and real going is possible. The church makes it easier and more effective for you to obey the instruction of Jesus when the mission of the whole church is clearly focused on sending.

2. Adopt gospel workers that you can individually partner with over a number of years. Make it a personal goal to know some of the workers that your church supports or others who you have been introduced to. Pray for them, read their updates, send them birthday gifts, and mobilizing other workers to join them. Know their work well and ask God to help you resource them to the best of your ability.

Q. Where could you discover people to support?

BEING PURPOSEFUL

1. Go to joshuaproject.org (or download the app) and do some research into people groups that are still unreached. Read the article https://joshuaproject.net/resources/articles/what_is_a_people_group and identify a people group on the site to begin to pray for.

2. Join your church's missionary support team. Most churches have some way that they keep up with missionaries and church planters that they support. Find out how you can get involved in helping those you support in a more personal way.

3. Go on a mission trip. Participating in a trip where you can see the work being done and gain a real heart for the people serving in the region will change the way you see missions. If you have never personally participated in a support trip we recommend that you do so as soon as possible.

Q. Is there an idea above that interests you? What can you do to take action immediately?

Rhythm 10: GOING

Summary: The Great Commission cannot be accomplished without our willingness to *go*. The spread of the gospel is not passive work; it is work that Jesus has clearly already sent us for. We must *go* into our daily lives understanding that we are the mission team for our local community. Furthermore, we must regularly consider whether we are to individually *go* into unreached contexts **rather than stay in more resourced areas**.

John 20:19-22. [19] On the evening of that day, the first day of the week, the doors being locked where the disciples were for fear of the Jews, Jesus came and stood among them and said to them, "Peace be with you." [20] When he had said this, he showed them his hands and his side. Then the disciples were glad when they saw the Lord. [21] Jesus said to them again, "Peace be with you. As the Father has sent me, even so I am sending you." [22] And when he had said this, he breathed on them and said to them, "Receive the Holy Spirit. (ESV)

Acts 1:6-8. [6] So when they had come together, they asked him, "Lord, will you at this time restore the kingdom to Israel?" [7] He said to them, "It is not for you to know times or seasons that the Father has fixed by his own authority. [8] But you will receive power when the Holy Spirit has come upon you, and you will be my witnesses in Jerusalem and in all Judea and Samaria, and to the end of the earth." (ESV)

2 Corinthians 5:18-21. [18] All this is from God, who through Christ reconciled us to himself and gave us the ministry of reconciliation; [19] that is, in Christ God was reconciling the world to himself, not counting their trespasses against them, and entrusting to us the message of reconciliation. [20] Therefore, we are ambassadors for Christ, God making his appeal through us. We implore you on behalf of Christ, be reconciled to God. [21] For our sake he made him to be sin who knew no sin, so that in him we might become the righteousness of God. (ESV)

BIBLICAL PRINCIPLES

1. Jesus has already "sent" his disciples. Understanding that we are to actively go to people with the gospel is a basic step of living as a disciple of Jesus. The question is not primarily "Am I sent?" but rather, "Who am I currently sent to?" The commission has been given.

We've been received into God's family by faith in Christ, therefore we've **joined the family business of reconciling people to God** through faith in Jesus Christ. *That means God has sovereignly sent you to the place you are now.* It is your responsibility to go into your community with a mindset that you are a witness to the power of the gospel! You are to join God in how He is working around you. The only question that remains is whether you should go to a place where there is *less* access to the gospel.

Q. How would accepting your identity as "**sent**" to your local community change the way you go about your daily life?

2. Christians will not accomplish our assigned commission unless more of us GO.
Jesus understood what he was assigning His people to do. The church does not lack resources. It mostly lacks willing people who will abandon their pursuits in life to take up the mission of Jesus to reach the unreached. Consider the terminology used above. We are *"sent"* people. In our ministry to the world we are *"ambassadors."* What do ambassadors do? They go to places where their "people" are not represented and the serve as a voice for their kingdom.

3. The work of the Holy Spirit among us will cause us to be a going people. Jesus tells his disciples that when the Holy Spirit comes upon them, they will be his witnesses, even to the ends of the earth. One measure of spiritual growth in the midst of the lives that make up our church will be an increased willingness to *go*. When it is absent, we should be concerned. We should regularly pray for the Holy Spirit to cause us to go wherever the gospel needs to be heard. Even at great personal and corporate cost.

Q. What are some things that keep Christians from taking the Great Commission seriously and personally? *List them and evaluate them in light of the cross and promised resurrection.*

BASIC PRACTICES

1. Learn to think and act like a missionary where you live. The same tradecraft that is necessary in a cross-cultural setting can be developed and applied wherever you're at. Figure out what barriers there are to the spread of the gospel in your own community. Figure out what groups of people are not being effectively reached. Develop plans and begin to experiment with ideas for reaching people nobody else is making an effort to connect with.

Q. What could you do to share the gospel with the people on your street? If you wanted to do it effectively, what would you need to think through?

Q. What immigrant populations exist in your community from countries where the gospel cannot be freely preached?

2. Explore ways that you could find work in areas overseas that need the gospel using your current profession and skills. Many people think of "going" only in a traditional model of being a Pastor or missionary "over there". Because of that, they never consider the limitless opportunities that Christians of many professions can capitalize on. Imagine positioning your life in an unreached area for the sake of the gospel. Imagine the eternal impact.

3. Become aware of opportunities to GO serve among the unreached with partner organizations through your local church. Many people are uninformed about the opportunities to go serve among the unreached through missions agencies that partner with your local church. Take some time to learn about needs on the mission field by staying in regular contact with sending agencies that assist churches in the work.

What exploration trips have you heard about and been interested in participating in? Do you think short-term trips can help people envision going for a longer commitment? *Explain your answer.*

BEING PURPOSEFUL

1. Go to the International Mission Board website at imb.org/opportunity-finder and learn about opportunities to serve among the unreached. The IMB is an incredible missions sending partner to local churches. Through them there are limitless opportunities to be engaged in going to serve cross-culturally in unreached places. The opportunities include jobs where a variety of different professional skills would be a better background than pastoral training.

Q. What skillset do you currently have that might be a good platform for living overseas?

2. Talk to one of your church leaders about long-term missionary service. Every church has different partnerships they have built to facilitate missions sending. There are often good opportunities to explore further about how you could be involved serving globally to carry the gospel to the unreached.

NOTES:

www.ingramcontent.com/pod-product-compliance
Lightning Source LLC
Chambersburg PA
CBHW081243020426
42331CB00013B/3285